W9-CBS-751

Amazing Animals
Snakes

Please visit our web site at www.garethstevens.com
For a free catalog describing our list of high-quality books, call 1-800-542-2595 (USA) or 1-800-387-3178 (Canada).
Our fax: 1-877-542-2596

Library of Congress Cataloging-in-Publication Data

Wilsdon, Christina.
    Snakes / by Christina Wilsdon.—U.S. ed.
            p. cm.—(Amazing Animals)
        Originally published: Pleasantville, NY: Reader's Digest Young Familiies, c2007.
        Includes bibliographical references and index.
        ISBN-10: 0-8368-9102-3   ISBN-13: 978-0-8368-9102-7 (lib. bdg.)
    1. Snakes—Juvenile literature. I. Title.
    QL666.O6W459 2009
    597.96—dc22   2008013382

This edition first published in 2009 by
Gareth Stevens Publishing
A Weekly Reader® Company
1 Reader's Digest Road
Pleasantville, NY 10570-7000 USA

This edition copyright © 2009 by Gareth Stevens, Inc. Original edition copyright © 2006 by Reader's Digest Young Families,
Pleasantville, NY 10570

Gareth Stevens Senior Managing Editor: Lisa M. Herrington
Gareth Stevens Creative Director: Lisa Donovan
Gareth Stevens Art Director: Ken Crossland
Gareth Stevens Associate Editor: Amanda Hudson

Consultant: Robert E. Budliger (Retired), NY State Department of Environmental Conservation

Credits
Cover: Timothy Craig Lubcke/Shutterstock Inc., Title page: Timothy Craig Lubcke/Shutterstock Inc., Contents: Mike Rogal/Shutterstock Inc., pages 6-7: Pam Burley/Shutterstock Inc., pages 8, 10, and 12: Dreamstime.com/Bruce Macqueen, pages 14-15: Brad Thompson/Shutterstock Inc., page 16: Morozova Tatiana/Shutterstock Inc., page 19: Coral Coolahan/Shutterstock Inc., page 20: Casey K. Bishop/Shutterstock Inc., pages 22-23: Rose Thompson/Shutterstock Inc., page 24: JupiterImages, page 27: EcoPrint/Shutterstock Inc., pages 28, 30, and 31: Photodisc/Getty Images, page 32: Timothy Craig Lubcke/Shutterstock Inc., page 33: Dreamstime.com/Robert Adrian Hillman, page 35 (large picture): Dreamstime.com/Olga Martelet, page 35 (inset): Dreamstime.com/Steffen Foerster, page 36 (large picture): Stephen Mcsweeny/Shutterstock Inc., page 36 (inset): Dreamstime.com/Nico Smit, pages 38-39: Morozova Tatiana/Shutterstock Inc., page 41: Carlos Arguelles/Shutterstock Inc., page 43: Bobby Deal/RealDealPhoto/Shutterstock Inc., pages 44-45: Dreamstime.com/Supersport, page 46: Dreamstime.com/Nico Smit, Back cover: Dynamic Graphics, Inc.

Printed in the United States of America

1 2 3 4 5 6 7 8 9 10 09

Amazing Animals

Snakes

By Christina Wilsdon

Gareth Stevens
Publishing

A WEEKLY READER COMPANY

Contents

Chapter 1
A Snake Story

About Garter Snakes

Garter snakes live in North America and Mexico. The kind found most often is the common garter snake. Garter snakes have different markings — but almost all of them have stripes on their backs and sides. Brown and yellow are common colors.

Most garter snakes **hibernate**, or go into a deep sleep, in winter. Hundreds of snakes pile into one den in late fall. With all those snakes packed into one cozy spot, the den's temperature stays above freezing all winter.

The garter snake laid in the spring sunshine. She had spent the winter coiled up in a **den** under rocks. Many other garter snakes had been there too. Now she was out of the den. The sun's rays warmed her body.

She was ready to stretch after being cramped up for so long. So were all the other garter snakes. Like her, those snakes were females. The males had left the den a week earlier.

The female snakes were hungry, but they first had to find mates. It was easy to find a mate now, while all the snakes were still close by.

The garter snake flicked her tongue in and out to "smell" the other snakes. Her tongue tapped on a spot on the ground. The scent on this spot was left by a male garter snake. She decided to follow his trail.

Snakes Are Reptiles

A **reptile** is a cold-blooded animal, which means that the temperature of its body is controlled by the temperature of the air or water around it. Lizards, turtles, and alligators are also reptiles.

After mating, the female snake **slithered** into a clump of bushes. The eggs would grow inside the female's body until it was time for the baby snakes to hatch.

The female snake flicked her tongue in and out as she searched for something to eat. She hadn't had a meal since last fall. She was hungry!

Like most garter snakes, the female snake ate anything small enough to catch. Her breakfast might be a slug or a worm. A small lizard or mouse would also make a nice meal.

The garter snake slid over the ground. Her stripes seemed to blend into the shadows. She was well hidden, but she was still careful to watch out for danger. A hungry crow might grab her!

Enemy Alert!

Common garter snakes are a favorite food of many animals. Hawks, crows, roadrunners, minks, opossums, skunks, raccoons, and cats are all natural **predators** of garter snakes. King snakes aren't much bigger than garter snakes, but they still like to eat them!

Baby Snakes

Garter snakes give birth to live young, so they are called live-bearers. But most snakes do not keep their eggs in their bodies. They lay eggs instead. The baby snakes grow inside the eggs, which are protected by a shell. The eggs are laid in a warm, moist place, such as under a log. Most snakes lay their eggs and leave them. But some kinds of snakes, like cobras, stay close to their eggs to protect them.

All spring and summer, the garter snake roamed the woods. She rested in the sun on a rock each morning. Then she hunted for food. Sometimes she found a tasty frog in a nearby stream. If she felt in danger, she slipped into the water and swam away.

By late summer, the baby snakes were ready to be born. The garter snake found a safe spot to have her babies. First the eggs hatched inside her body. Then the baby snakes were born. Altogether, the mother snake gave birth to 25 babies!

The mother garter snake stayed near her babies for a while. But she did not have to do anything to care for them. The baby snakes were on their own from the start. Soon they began crawling away to find food.

The mother garter snake slithered off to look for a meal too. She needed to fatten up for the winter. She would stop eating about two weeks before slipping back into the winter den in November. And there she would stay, waiting for spring to come again.

Chapter 2
The Body of a Snake

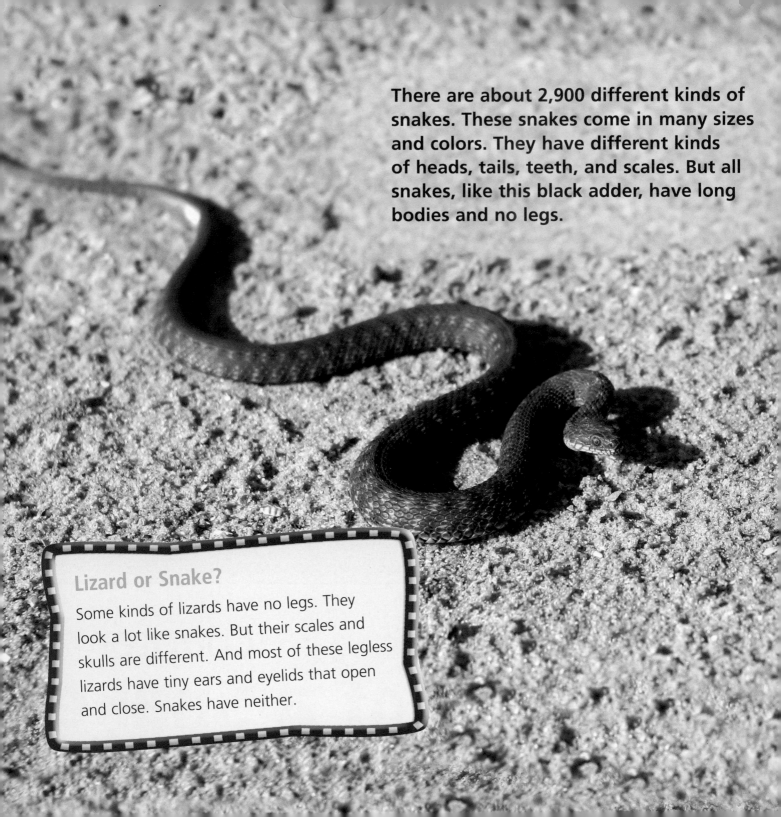

There are about 2,900 different kinds of snakes. These snakes come in many sizes and colors. They have different kinds of heads, tails, teeth, and scales. But all snakes, like this black adder, have long bodies and no legs.

Lizard or Snake?

Some kinds of lizards have no legs. They look a lot like snakes. But their scales and skulls are different. And most of these legless lizards have tiny ears and eyelids that open and close. Snakes have neither.

Snaky Motions

A snake gets around very well without legs. It uses its entire body to move. A snake's body is a long backbone with many pairs of ribs all wrapped around with muscle.

A snake can bend its body into curves to wriggle along the ground. This motion is often called slithering. The snake pushes the curves of its body against the ground, or against objects like plants and stones.

Another motion snakes use is called concertina locomotion. A snake moving in this way coils its hind end and reaches forward with its head and the front of its body. Then it places its head and front end on the ground and pulls up the hind end of its body.

A snake can also travel in a straight line by moving the sections of its scaly belly skin forward and back. The sections simply move one after the other, "hitching" the snake forward.

Some snakes move across sand by going sideways. A snake moves this way by looping its front part to one side. Then it throws its hind end to the same side to catch up with its front end. This motion is called **sidewinding**.

Skin and Scales

A snake's body is covered with skin that is also covered with thicker patches of skin called **scales**. The scales overlap each other so that they hide the underskin. But when a snake stretches and the scales move apart, the skin underneath can be seen. Scales come in many shapes and sizes.

Shedding Skin

A snake sheds the entire outer layer of its skin at once. It sheds its skin so it can grow larger and get rid of a worn-out skin. Some kinds of snakes shed their skin several times a year.

When a snake is ready to shed, its body makes a liquid that spreads under the skin's outer layer. This makes its skin colors look dull and its eyes look milky. The snake rubs its nose on objects and on the ground to help peel off the skin. The skin slides off the snake's body inside-out in one piece. After shedding the outer skin, the fresh skin underneath looks bright and new.

Many people think the skin of a snake will feel damp and slimy. But a snake's skin feels dry.

Hot and Cold

Snakes are cold-blooded. This means their body does not heat up from the inside like yours does. Snakes warm up by lying in sunlight. They may also lie on a warm surface, such as a rock. To cool off, a snake moves to a shady spot.

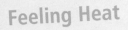

Feeling Heat

Some snakes, such as rattlesnakes, can find warm-blooded animals (such as mice and birds) by sensing body heat. The snake senses the heat with pits on its head. A snake can catch **prey** in total darkness in this way.

Snakes that are active by day, like this hognose snake, have good color vision. Snakes that are active at night have good black-and-white vision.

Snake Eyes

Snakes do not have eyelids that open and shut. Instead, most snakes have a single, clear scale over each eye for protection. A snake's eyes are good at spotting motion. But they are not very good at seeing details or anything sitting still.

Are Snakes Deaf?

A snake does not have ears, and it can't hear most sounds that travel through air. But it does have small ear bones in its head. These bones are linked to the snake's lower jaw. The snake's jaw is able to sense the vibrations of some sounds that travel through the ground.

Sensing Smells

A snake can pick up scents with its nose, but it also "smells" with its tongue. It flicks its tongue out to "taste" the air. It also touches the ground and other objects with its tongue. Then the snake pushes its tongue into a special part of the roof of its mouth. This part works with the nostrils and the brain to figure out what the snake has found. The snake uses this sense to find food.

Chapter 3
Snake Life

Catching Prey

Many types of snakes sit and wait for prey. When the prey comes near, the snake attacks it. Some snakes wiggle their brightly colored tail tips to attract prey to step closer.

Other snakes hunt. They crawl along branches or the ground, flicking out their tongues to sense prey. Then they creep up on it. Hunting snakes may drop out of trees and land on top of their next meal!

Eating Prey

Different kinds of snakes have different ways of killing their prey. Pythons and boas hold prey in their jaws and wrap their bodies around it. Every time the prey breathes out, the snake tightens its coils a bit more. This is called **constriction**.

Some snakes kill prey with poison called **venom**. The venom comes out of their fangs when they bite. The snakes usually wait for the prey to die before eating it.

To swallow food, most snakes open their jaws wide. First the snake surrounds the prey with its jaws and hooks its teeth into it. Then the snake moves its jaws, one side at a time, over the prey. It is as if the jaws "walk" across the prey.

Snake Menus

Snakes eat many different kinds of foods. Their meals may include worms, insects, spiders, slugs, snails, eggs, fish, frogs, lizards, other snakes, turtles, birds, and small mammals. Some snakes can even swallow animals as big as gazelles!

A brown house snake finishes a rat. This snake is very common around the cities and towns of southern Africa.

Snakes on the Menu

Many animals—including skunks and eagles, opossums and owls—eat snakes. Crocodiles and lizards prey on snakes, too. King cobras and king snakes eat other snakes. A king snake can even devour a rattlesnake. It is not harmed by the rattler's venom!

The black-and-yellow mangrove snake can be found in areas of Southeast Asia. It lives in trees and on land. It likes to catch birds at night.

Hiss, Rattle, and Stink!

Snakes escape from or scare off their predators in many ways. If a snake is cornered, it will defend itself. Some snakes make themselves look big and scary. The bullsnake snorts, grunts, and hisses. A rattlesnake curls up and rattles its tail.

Some snakes have brightly colored tails or undersides. They can reveal them suddenly by twisting. The color can surprise a predator and give the snake time to escape. Some snakes have tails that break off if they are grabbed.

Some snakes play dead. If a hognose snake is attacked, it goes limp and lets its tongue dangle. It also releases a smelly fluid, which may force the enemy to leave.

A predator that ignores warnings might be bitten. This means trouble if the snake is venomous, or poisonous. Spitting cobras of Asia and Africa can spray their venom 8 feet (2.4 meters) through the air, right into an enemy's eyes!

Chapter 4
Kinds of Snakes

The green tree python coils its body around a tree branch.

It's Easy Being Green

The green tree python lives in the **rainforests** of Australia and the nearby island of New Guinea. Young tree pythons are bright yellow or red when they are babies. These colors help them hide among flowers. The pythons turn green when they are about six months old. This snake grows up to 6 feet (1.8 m) long. It hunts lizards, bats, and other animals it finds in trees. Pits on its lips sense heat and help it find prey.

The Biggest Snake?

The reticulated (ruh TIK yu lay ted) python lives in Southeast Asia. It is often called the world's longest snake. The longest reticulated python was nearly 33 feet (10 m) — about the length of a school bus!

A reticulated python's skin has patches of brown and tan. Its coloring helps it hide in a tree or on the forest floor. The python seizes its prey, coils its body around it, and squeezes it to death.

Vivid Viper

The eyelash palm pit viper is a venomous snake. It lives in trees in Central America and part of South America. It grows to be about 30 inches (76 centimeters) long. The viper comes in many colors, including yellow, green, gray, and even orange. Some have black, white, or red spots.

The viper's "eyelashes" are really pointy scales that stick up from above its eyes. The scales may help protect its eyes, or break up the shape of its head to confuse enemies.

The eyelash palm pit viper hunts for prey with the help of heat-sensitive pits on its face. The pits help it sense mice, birds, frogs, and lizards. The viper wraps its tail around a branch. Then it lunges the rest of its body at its prey.

Most venomous snakes bite their prey, then let go and wait for the venom to kill it. But this viper hangs on to the prey while it waits for its venom to work. That way, its meal doesn't fall out of the tree!

The eyelash palm pit viper keeps out of sight during the day. But it hunts all night, from early evening until dawn.

A Horned Snake

The rhinoceros viper gets its name from the pointy scales at the end of its snout. They stick up like a rhinoceros's horns. Scientists are trying to find out what the viper's "horns" do.

Hooded Snake

The Cape cobra lives in dry lands in southern Africa. Like all cobras, it makes itself look bigger when it is threatened. It raises the front part of its body off the ground. Then it flares its **hood**. The hood is formed by ribs in the cobra's neck that lift and spread to stretch out its skin. Then the cobra hisses loudly.

A rattlesnake can rattle its tail from 20 to 100 times per second!

Snake in the Grass

There are about 30 different kinds of rattlesnakes. Most of them are found in North America. The most common type of rattlesnake is the western rattlesnake. It is sometimes called the prairie rattlesnake because it lives in grasslands, or prairies. The western rattlesnake can grow to be 4 feet (1.2 m) long.

Like all rattlesnakes, the western rattlesnake's bite is venomous. Its fangs fold up and fit inside the snake's mouth when it is closed. They lie against the top of the mouth. When the rattlesnake strikes, its jaws open and the long fangs snap forward. The venom flows out of glands in the snake's head and through the fangs when it bites.

The rattlesnake is named for the rattle on its tail. This rattle is made of tough sections of skin that are loosely connected to each other. The tail makes a loud, buzzing sound when the rattlesnake shakes it. A rattlesnake rattles to warn enemies away. It also rattles to warn off big animals that might accidentally step on it.

Chapter 5
Snakes in the World

Snakes and People

Throughout history, people from all over the world have had different ideas about snakes. In some cultures, snakes have been honored. In others, snakes have been feared and disliked.

In ancient Egypt, the snake was a symbol of rain and good crops. The people honored a goddess who looked like a cobra. They even kept cobras in their temples. People in India also worshiped cobras.

The ancient Greeks thought snakes were sacred, too. They believed that snakes lived forever. This belief led to the use of snakes as a symbol for doctors. This symbol is still used in many countries today.

Snakes also wriggle through many stories from ancient times. People in part of Africa believed that a snake carried the world on its back. The Hopi Indians of North America believed snakes carried their wish for rain to the rain gods.

In many parts of Europe, people thought that snakes were evil creatures. This belief still exists in many places. It has led many people to think of snakes as "bad" animals.

Snakes Are Everywhere!

Snakes live on all continents except Antarctica. They can be found in different **habitats**. Snakes live in tropical rain forests and deserts, woodlands and grasslands, swamps and marshes. Some kinds of snakes live in freshwater, while others live in the salty ocean.

Snakes have slithered across the world for at least 120 million years, since the time when dinosaurs still existed. Some scientists are finding clues that show snakes may be even older.

The Future of Snakes

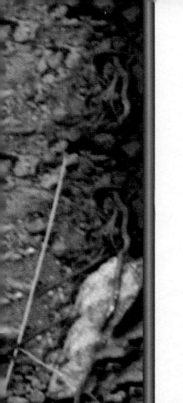

The biggest threat to snakes is the loss of habitat. Snakes have less space when forests are cut down and wetlands are drained.

Another threat to snakes is the use of their skins to make shoes and other items. Some snakes are raised on "snake farms" to provide snakeskin. But millions of wild snakes are illegally killed for their skins every year.

One law that has helped protect snakes is the Convention on International Trade in Endangered Species. This law makes it illegal to sell certain kinds of animals or their body parts. It was signed in 1973 by 80 countries. Since then, other countries have signed this agreement, too.

Fast Facts About Garter Snakes

Scientific name	*Thamnophis sirtalis*
Class	Reptilia
Order	Squamata
Size	18 to 54 inches (46 to 137 cm)
Life span	Up to 2 years in the wild Up to 10 years in captivity
Habitat	Fields, wetlands, woods; near lakes, streams; gardens, farms

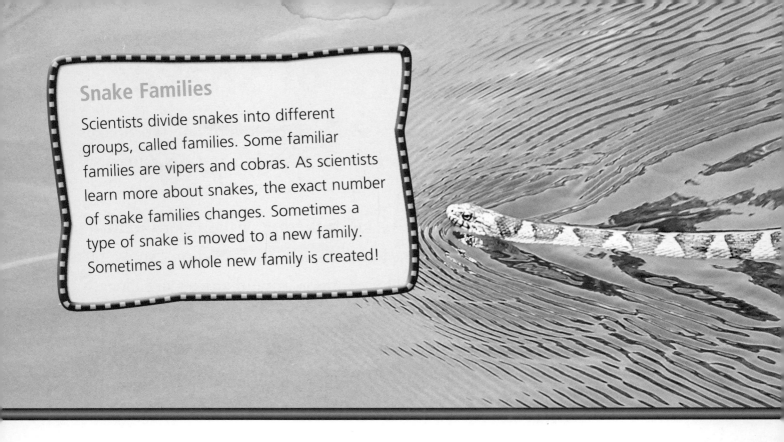

Snake Families

Scientists divide snakes into different groups, called families. Some familiar families are vipers and cobras. As scientists learn more about snakes, the exact number of snake families changes. Sometimes a type of snake is moved to a new family. Sometimes a whole new family is created!

Glossary

constriction — a snake's way of killing prey by tightening its coils around the prey's body

den — place where a wild animal sleeps or rests

habitat — the natural environment where an animal or plant lives

hibernate — to go into a deep sleep all winter

hood — the ribs and skin that a cobra can stretch open on its neck to make itself look bigger

predator — an animal that hunts and eats other animals to survive

prey — animals that are hunted by other animals for food

rain forest — a hot, humid tropical forest where it rains frequently

reptile — a cold-blooded animal that's body temperature is controlled by the temperature of the air or water around it

scales — thickened patches of skin on a snake's body

sidewinding — a looping sideways motion used by snakes to cross hot sand

slithering — the wriggling motion a snake makes to move along the ground

venom — a poisonous fluid produced by some snakes that is released when the snake bites its prey

Snakes:
Show What You Know

How much have you learned about snakes? Grab
a piece of paper and a pencil and write your answers down.

1. Why are garter snakes called live-bearers?

2. About how many different kinds of snakes are there?

3. Why does a snake shed its skin?

4. How far can the spitting cobras of Asia and Africa spray their venom?

5. What color is the green tree python when it is a baby?

6. What are the "eyelashes" of the eyelash palm pit viper made of?

7. How does the reticulated python kill its prey?

8. Which type of rattlesnake is the most common?

9. What were snakes a symbol for in ancient Egypt?

10. What is the biggest threat to today's snakes?

1. Because they give birth to live young 2. 2,900 3. So that it can grow larger and get rid of a worn-out skin 4. 8 feet (2.4 m) 5. Red or yellow 6. Pointy scales 7. By squeezing it to death 8. The western (or prairie) rattlesnake 9. Rain and good crops 10. The loss of habitat

For More Information

Books

Snakes. Animal Lives (series). Morgan, Sally (QEB Publishing, 2005)

Snakes. Zoobooks (series). Wexo, John Bonnett (Wildlife Education, Ltd., 2001)

Snakes and Lizards: What They Have in Common. Animals in Order (series). Miller, Sara Swan (Franklin Watts, 2000)

Web Sites

Reptiles

http://netvet.wustl.edu/reptiles.htm#snake

Check out the snake page for the Electronic Zoo. You'll find links to cool snake sites, facts, and fun.

Reptiles: Snake

http://www.sandiegozoo.org/animalbytes/t-snake.html

Meet Nyoka, Big Tex, and other beloved San Diego Zoo snakes. Read all about these reptiles and their relatives.

Publisher's note to educators and parents: Our editors have carefully reviewed these web sites to ensure that they are suitable for children. Many web sites change frequently, however, and we cannot guarantee that a site's future contents will continue to meet our high standards of quality and educational value. Be advised that children should be closely supervised whenever they access the Internet.

Index